SIMPLE MACHINES

By • DEBORAH • HODGE

PHOTOGRAPHS BY RAY BOUDREAU

KIDS CAN PRESS

3-01
CH

Acknowledgements

I would like to gratefully acknowledge the review of my manuscript by Gary McKinnon. Thanks also to my husband and children for their unending supply of ideas, advice and encouragement.
— Deborah Hodge

First U.S. edition 1998
Text copyright © 1996 by Deborah Hodge
Photographs copyright © 1996 by Ray Boudreau

Published in Canada by
Kids Can Press Ltd.
29 Birch Avenue
Toronto, ON M4V 1E2

Published in the U.S. by
Kids Can Press Ltd.
85 River Rock Drive, Suite 202
Buffalo, NY 14207

Edited by Valerie Wyatt
Designed by James Ireland

Printed in Hong Kong by Wing King Tong Company Limited

CMC   96 0 9 8 7 6 5 4 3
CM PA 98 0 9 8 7 6 5 4 3 2

Canadian Cataloguing in Publication Data

Hodge, Deborah
    Simple machines

(Starting with science)
Includes index.

ISBN 1-55074-311-2 (bound)   1-55074-399-6 (pbk.)

1. Simple machines — Experiments — Juvenile literature. 2. Simple machines — Juvenile literature. I. Boudreau, Ray. II. Title. III. Series.

TJ147.H63 1996   j621.8'11   C96-930723-3

Kids Can Press is a Nelvana company

Table of contents

Table trick

Can you lift a friend without touching him? You can with the help of a simple machine.

You will need:
- a small table
- a sturdy straight-backed chair
- a strong broomstick (or a rake handle or hockey stick)

What to do:
1. Ask a friend to sit or lie on the table near one edge and hold on. Grab on to the edge of the table and try to lift it and your friend. Is this hard to do?

2. Put the chair near the table with its seat facing away.

3. Lay the broomstick over the chair back. Wedge one end of the stick under the table top.

4. Put one knee on the chair seat to hold it down. Slowly push down on the free end of the broomstick. What happens?

5. Try moving the chair closer or farther from the table. Is lifting the table easier or harder?

What's happening?
When you push down on one end of the broomstick, your pushing power is changed into a strong lifting power at the other end.

A lever
The broomstick is working as a lever — a type of simple machine. A lever is any stiff bar that turns on a resting point called a fulcrum. (In this case, the fulcrum is the back of the chair.) The lever helps you lift heavy things by turning your pushing force into a smaller but more powerful lifting movement.

Simple machines
A lever is one of six simple machines. The others are: the wheel and axle, the pulley, the inclined plane, the screw and the wedge. Simple machines don't need electricity to work — only the power of your muscles. Simple machines make tough jobs easier by changing the power, speed or direction of a movement.

Balancing act

Have you ever played on a teeter-totter? Here's a trick that will show you how to lift two friends all by yourself.

You will need:
- scissors
- the cardboard tube from a roll of toilet paper
- a ruler
- some building blocks (or sugar cubes or pennies)

What to do:
1. Cut the cardboard tube in half, lengthwise. Place one piece on a table, cut part down.

2. Set the ruler on top. Put a block on each end of the ruler. Can you make them balance?

3. Pile more blocks on one end of the ruler. How many blocks can you lift with just one block on the other end? **Hint:** Try changing the position of the cardboard tube or the pile of blocks.

What's happening?
Your ruler is working as a lever. The longer the distance between the single block and the cardboard tube (the fulcrum), the more blocks you can lift. To lift two friends on a teeter-totter (also a lever), sit far away from the fulcrum (the middle) and have your friends sit near it.

Wacky wheels

If you have taken a ride on a bike or wagon, you'll know that wheels help you go places. How? Make this toy car and find out.

You will need:

- an empty cardboard milk carton, 1 L (1 quart) size
- scissors
- a long smooth board
- some thick books
- 2 long colored pencils
- 4 large thread spools

What to do:

1. Cut the milk carton in half lengthwise to make two cars.
2. Raise one end of the board on a pile of books. Place one car at the top of the board ramp. What happens?
3. Ask an adult to use the scissors to poke holes at the front and back of the other car. Each hole should be about the size of a dime.

4. Slide a colored pencil through the front holes. Slide another colored pencil through the back holes.
5. Push a spool onto the end of each colored pencil. Leave a small space between the spool and the outside of the car.
6. Put the car at the top of the ramp again and let it go.

What's happening?

Without wheels, your car can't move. There's too much friction (rubbing) between it and the ground. Wheels reduce the amount of friction so that your car can zoom down the ramp.

A wheel and axle

When you combine a wheel (the spool) with an axle (the colored pencil), you have a simple machine called a wheel and axle. You can move heavy objects by putting a wheel and axle under them.

Candy collector

Can you lift a candy just by blowing?

You will need:

- scissors
- a piece of colored construction paper
- a pencil and ruler
- tape
- a long colored pencil
- an empty cardboard milk carton
- a piece of string 30 cm (1 foot) long
- a Life Savers candy

What to do:

1. Cut out a square piece of construction paper 18 x 18 cm (7 x 7 inches) and mark it as shown.

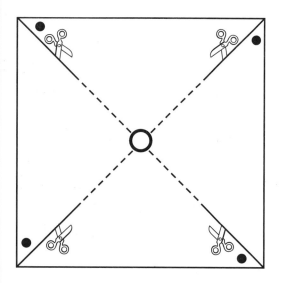

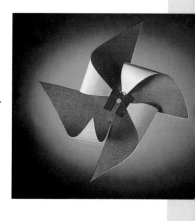

2. Starting at one corner, cut halfway down the pencil line. Do the same for the other corners.

3. Fold one dotted corner point over so that it just touches the center circle. Tape it down. Do the same with the three other dotted corner points.

4. Ask an adult to poke a hole through the center circle. Slide the colored pencil through the hole.

5. Cut off the top of the milk carton and cut two slots as shown.

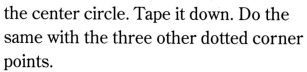

6. Tie one end of the string to the candy. Tie the other end to the colored pencil and tape it in place. Set the pencil in the milk carton slots.

7. Hold on to the base of the windmill and blow on the sails. Can you make them turn? What happens to the candy?

What's happening?

Your windmill is a wheel and axle machine. The paper wheel and pencil axle change the forward movement of your breath into a turning movement. The turning causes the string to wind up and lift the candy.

Bubble race

Challenge a friend to see who can whip up the biggest batch of bubbles in the shortest time.

You will need:
- 2 mixing bowls of the same size
- liquid dish soap
- a teaspoon
- a mixing spoon
- a rotary eggbeater
- a clock or watch that shows seconds

What to do:
1. Half fill each bowl with water.
2. Pour a teaspoon of dish soap into each bowl. Do not stir.
3. Give your friend the mixing spoon. You will use the eggbeater. Starting at the same time, use your mixing tools to whip up the soap and water. Mix as fast as you can for 30 seconds. Who makes the most bubbles?

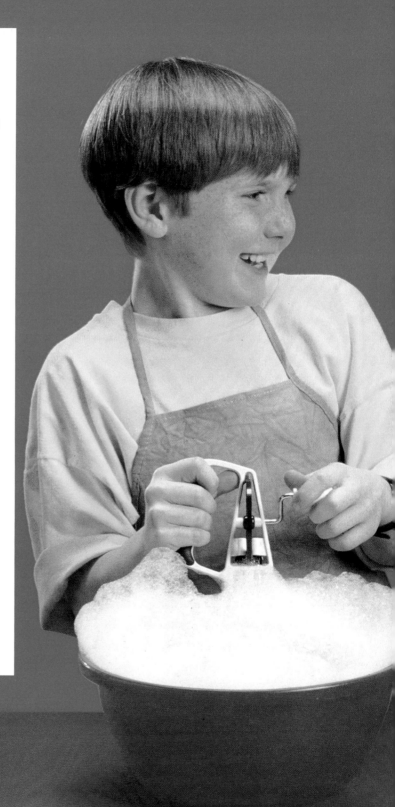

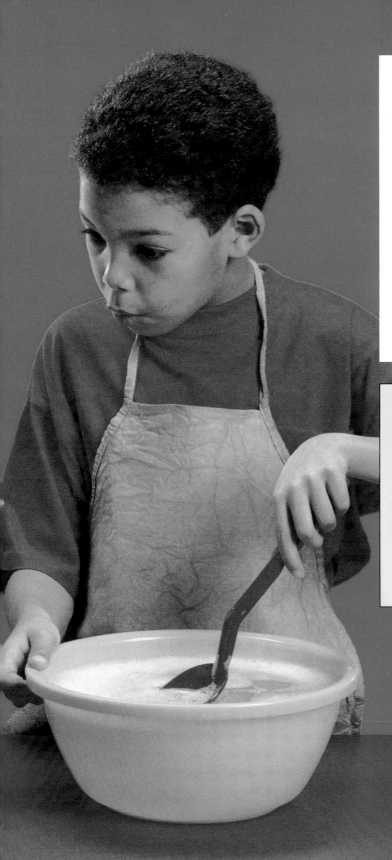

What's happening?

The eggbeater is a wheel and axle machine. It is made up of wheels that work together, called gears. When you turn the handle, a large wheel moves smaller gear wheels. As the small gears turn, they make the beaters spin fast. The gears change the force of your hand movement into a faster motion. This helps you whip up the most bubbles in the shortest time.

Gears

Gears are wheels with teeth that turn and work together. Different sizes and arrangements of gears do different jobs. A large gear turning smaller ones will give you more speed. A small gear turning large ones will give you more power.

Going up!

What do you call a wheel that turns on a rope and lifts heavy weights? A pulley. How does it work? Make this toy elevator and see.

You will need:

- a piece of string 60 cm (2 feet) long
- a small empty thread spool
- clear adhesive tape
- some heavy books
- 1 m (3 feet) of ribbon (wide enough to fit snugly between the rims of the thread spool)
- a plastic bucket
- small objects to lift

What to do:

1. Thread the string through the center hole of the thread spool.
2. Tape the ends of the string to a table top so that the spool hangs about 10 cm (4 inches) below the table's edge. Use heavy books to hold the string ends in place.

3. Tie one end of the ribbon to the handle of the bucket.
4. Slide the free end of the ribbon over the thread spool. Slowly pull down on the free end. What happens to the bucket?
5. Place small objects in your bucket elevator. Try lifting them.

What's happening?

When you pull *down* on the ribbon, the bucket lifts *up*. The toy elevator changes your pulling movement into a lifting movement.

A pulley

When you combine a wheel (in this case, the spool) with a rope (the ribbon), you have a pulley. A pulley can change the direction of the force exerted by your muscles. Instead of lifting a heavy object straight up, you pull down on a rope attached to it. Pulling down is easier because you can use the weight of your body to help you.

Pulling power

Invite your friends to a pulling contest and surprise them with your strength.

You will need:
- a piece of rope about 3 m (9 feet) long
- 2 broomsticks (or rake handles)

What to do:
1. Knot one end of the rope to the end of a broomstick.

2. Ask your friends to stand facing each other about 30 cm (1 foot) apart. Give them each a broomstick. Tell them to hold the broomsticks parallel — the same distance apart at both ends.

3. Loop the rope around the broomsticks as shown.

4. Challenge your friends to hold the broomsticks apart while you pull hard on the free end of the rope. Who wins?

What's happening?
Chances are you were able to pull the broomsticks together. Why? The rope and broomsticks act as a moveable pulley. The pulley multiplies the force of your muscles, giving you extra pulling power.

When you're ready to try this trick, lift the sticks off the floor.

Egg drop

Ever wanted to drop an egg and watch what happens? Here's your chance!

You will need:

- 2 eggs (Warning: the eggs may break. Substitute hard-boiled eggs, if you wish.)
- 2 food cans 8 cm (3 inches) tall
- scissors
- an empty box from aluminum foil or plastic food wrap
- adhesive tape

What to do:

1. Hold an egg in one hand. Rest the hand on top of a can as the boy is doing in the picture. Let the egg drop. Does it crack?
2. Cut off the lid and one end of the box.
3. Make a ramp by taping the closed end of the box to the top of one can.
4. Place an egg at the top of the ramp and let it roll down. When the egg stops, check it.

What's happening?

The force of dropping the egg was so great that the shell cracked. When the egg rolled down the ramp, the force was less — not enough to crack it. The difference was the ramp. It is a simple machine that is sometimes called an inclined plane.

An inclined plane

An inclined plane allows you to lower (or lift) heavy objects using less force. But in order to use less force, you must move the object over a greater distance. Measure the length of the ramp. Now measure the height of the can. Which way does the egg have to travel farther — when it's dropped straight down or rolled along the ramp?

Penny lift

Have you ever run up a ramp? If so, you were using a simple machine called an inclined plane. Here's how to put an inclined plane to work.

You will need:

- some books
- a board or book at least 35 cm (14 inches) long
- a knife
- a small plastic yogurt container
- a piece of string 3 times as long as the board
- a toy car
- 20 or more marbles or pennies

What to do:

1. Put a small pile of books near the edge of a table. Rest one edge of the board on top. This is your ramp.

2. Ask an adult to poke two small holes near the top of the yogurt container, on opposite sides. Thread the string through the holes and tie it as shown.

3. Tie or tape the other end of the string to the toy car.
4. Set the car near the bottom of the ramp. Drape the string up over the board, so that the yogurt container hangs just over the edge of the board as shown.
5. Drop marbles or pennies, one at a time, into the container until the car moves to the top of the ramp. How many marbles or pennies does it take?
6. Make a steeper ramp by placing a taller stack of books under the board. Does it take more marbles or pennies to move the car to the top, or fewer?

What's happening?

The dropping marbles or pennies are the force that makes the car move. The steeper the inclined plane (the ramp), the more force (marbles or pennies) you must use.

Screwy water

Most water flows downhill. But not the water in this picture. It's flowing up! Try it yourself with the help of a simple machine.

You will need:

- a piece of plastic aquarium tubing 135 cm (4½ feet) long (available at pet stores)
- tape
- an empty can, the taller the better
- a mixing bowl
- food coloring

What to do:

1. Tape one end of the plastic tubing to the top of the can. Wind the tubing around the can in a spiral. The tubing should look something like the turns on a screw. Tape the end to the bottom of the can.

2. Half fill the bowl with water. Mix in a few drops of food coloring.
3. Place the top end of the can and tubing into the bowl. Slowly turn the can until colored water moves into the tubing.
4. Lift the can out of the bowl and tilt it slightly.
5. Slowly turn the can and watch what happens. If the water doesn't climb, try holding the can at a slightly different angle.

What's happening?

The spiral tubing makes it easier for the water to climb up. The tubing acts as a screw — a simple machine used to lift or move things.

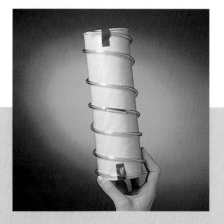

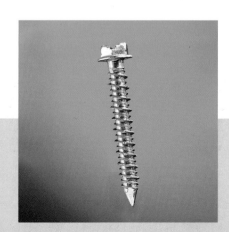

A screw

A screw is actually an inclined plane that winds around. Like an inclined plane, a screw allows you to move things using less force. By winding around, a screw (the tubing) makes a longer but more gentle slope for the water to move up.

Twirling toy

Make this toy helicopter and watch it fly. It's actually a simple machine that makes a soft landing every time.

You will need:

- a piece of paper 18 x 5 cm (7 x 2 inches)
- a pencil
- scissors
- a paper clip

What to do:

1. Lay the paper strip over the pattern below. Trace the solid cutting and dotted folding lines.

2. Cut the solid lines A and B. Fold along the dotted lines C and D. Fold along the dotted line E.

3. Slide a paper clip onto the folded tip.

4. Cut the solid line F. Bend flap G back and flap H forward as shown.

5. Lift your toy helicopter up high and let it go. How does it move? Try flying it from a higher spot.

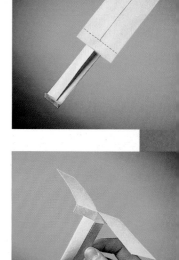

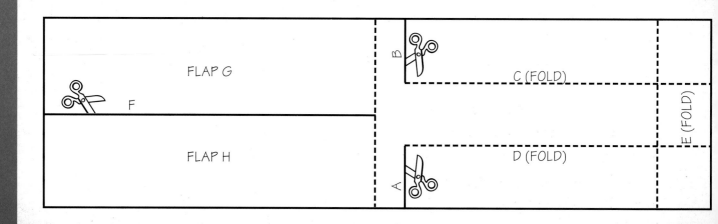

FLAP G

F

FLAP H

B

A

C (FOLD)

D (FOLD)

E (FOLD)

What's happening?

The toy helicopter twirls in a spiral as it drops. The twirling blades act as a screw — a simple machine that helps you lower (or lift) things with less force. Turning in a spiral allows the helicopter to drop with less force. It lands softly instead of crashing down.

Funny face

Make a funny fruit face. A simple machine will help you do it.

You will need:
- a paring knife
- a carrot
- an apple (choose a soft type such as a McIntosh)

What to do:
1. Ask an adult to slice the carrot into circles about 0.5 cm (¼ inch) thick.
2. Try pushing one carrot circle into the apple. What happens?

3. Cut another carrot circle into a point.
4. Push the point of the carrot into the apple. Which shape of carrot is easier to push in — the point or circle?
5. Cut the other carrot circles into points. Push them into the apple to make a funny face. Try other fruits and vegetables to make more funny creatures.

What's happening?
It's easier to push in the pointed piece of carrot because it acts as a wedge — a simple machine used to separate or split things.

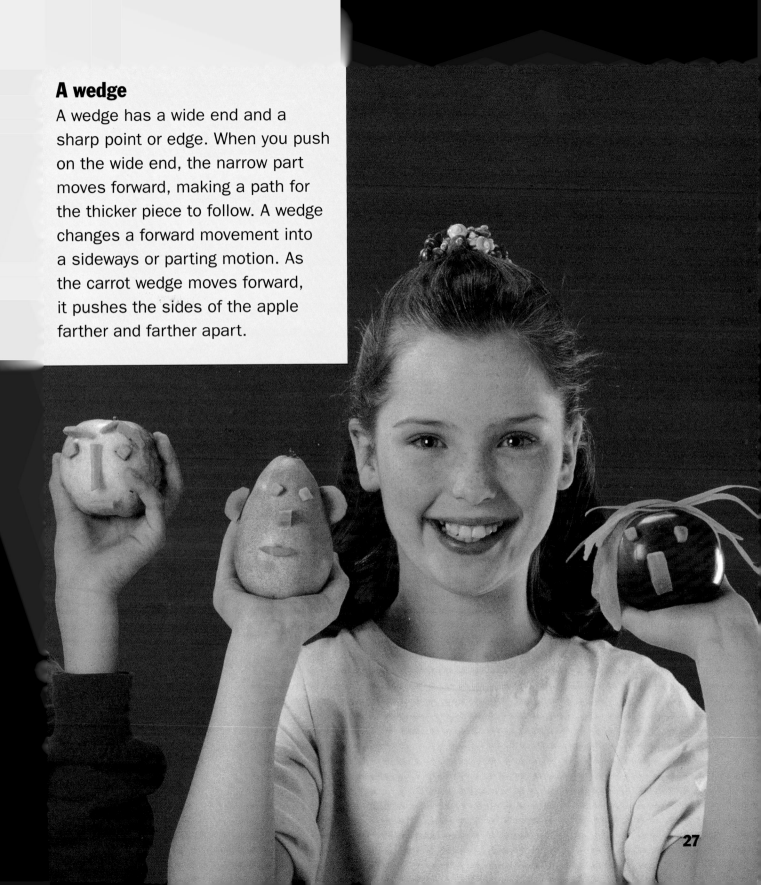

A wedge

A wedge has a wide end and a sharp point or edge. When you push on the wide end, the narrow part moves forward, making a path for the thicker piece to follow. A wedge changes a forward movement into a sideways or parting motion. As the carrot wedge moves forward, it pushes the sides of the apple farther and farther apart.

Mystery machine

In the mood to solve a mystery? Make this toy paddle boat to float in a bathtub or wading pool. While you're at it, try to figure out which two simple machines help the boat go.

You will need:

- scissors
- an empty cardboard milk carton, 1 L (1 quart) size
- 2 pencils
- 2 small rubber bands

What to do:

1. Cut the carton in half lengthwise. Use one half for the body of your boat.
2. Ask an adult to poke two holes in the flat bottom of the carton. Slide a pencil into each hole, leaving the ends sticking out 7 cm (about 3 inches).
3. Using the leftover carton half, cut a piece 7 x 3 cm (3 x 1 inch). This is the paddle for your boat.
4. Put one rubber band around the pencil ends inside the body of the boat. The rubber band will be loose.

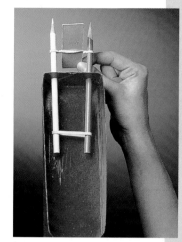

5. Put the other rubber band around the pencil ends sticking out of the boat. Slip the paddle between this rubber band and wind it up about 25 times.
6. Holding on to the paddle, place the boat in a bathtub or wading pool. Let it go and watch it paddle around.
Hint: If the boat goes backward, wind the paddle in the other direction.

What's happening?

Two simple machines are helping the boat go. At the front of the boat is a wedge. Can you see the wide part that narrows into a point? This is called the bow. A wedge-shaped bow helps a boat cut through the water. At the back of the boat, the paddle is a wheel turning on an rubber-band axle. As the paddle turns, it pushes or pulls the boat through the water.

For parents and teachers

The activities in this book are designed to teach children about the six simple machines: the lever, wheel and axle, pulley, inclined plane, screw and wedge. Simple machines do not save work, but they make tough jobs (such as lifting heavy objects) easier by changing the power, speed or direction of a force. Here are some ideas to extend the activities in the book.

Table trick

What else is a lever? Look for a bottle opener, shovel, crowbar, stapler, claw end of a hammer, pair of scissors, nutcrackers, tweezers or pliers. To see how these levers make work easier, try doing the same work without them.

Balancing act

How many more blocks can you lift if you increase the distance between the fulcrum and the single block? Repeat the experiment using a longer ruler.

Wacky wheels

Ask a child to sit on an upside-down wagon, then try to pull it. Turn the wagon upright and try again. Which way is easier? Sliding friction (without wheels) is greater than rolling friction (with wheels).

Candy collector

In a real windmill, the wind turns blades that revolve on an axle. The turning axle causes gears and other machine parts to move and do useful work, such as pumping water or grinding grain. How much weight can the candy collector lift? Try adding more Life Savers candies.

Bubble race

Working together, gears can change the strength, speed or direction of a movement. How do gears on a bicycle work? Flip a bicycle upside down, turn the pedals and watch the gears as you try a low gear, then higher gears. Try riding uphill and on level ground in different gears. Which gears work best for each?

Going up!

Have a pulley hunt. Look for pulleys on a clothesline, flag pole, crane, sailboat or fishing boat. What is each pulley moving?

Pulling power

Use a longer rope and make a few more loops around the broomsticks. Does this give more or less pulling power? (The more turns of the rope, the greater your power. But for every turn, the rope's pulling length must be increased.)

Egg drop and Penny lift

Try "Egg drop" using a steeper ramp. Does the egg have a harder or softer landing? Try "Penny lift" using a longer ramp. Does it take more or less force (more or fewer pennies) to move a car up a longer ramp? Look for other ramps in your neighborhood.

Screwy water and Twirling toy

A screw can help you lift or lower things with less force, but it also has another important use — as a strong fastener. Have a hunt to find screws used as fasteners. Look for a wood screw, corkscrew, metal end of a lightbulb, cup hook, large hook-style plant hanger, workbench vice, toothpaste cap and screw-on jar lid. What is each screw holding in place?

Funny face

Bite into an apple with your front teeth. Take another bite with your back teeth. Which teeth are sharper biters? (Your front teeth — because they are wedges.) What else is a wedge? A toothpick, pin, sewing needle, nail, axe, chisel, knife and scissor blades.

Mystery machine

Most machines are made up of a combination of two or more simple machines. Try inventing your own mystery machine by combining some simple machines. What work can you get your mystery machine to do?

Words to know

axle: a bar or rod that a wheel turns on

force: a push or pull on an object that causes it to change direction, move or stop

friction: the rubbing force of one object against another. Friction causes moving objects to slow down.

fulcrum: the resting or balance point upon which a lever turns

gear: a wheel with ridges or teeth. One gear connects and turns another.

inclined plane: a sloping surface used to move heavy loads up or down

lever: a stiff bar that turns on a fulcrum and is used to move heavy loads

pulley: a wheel with a groove that a rope or wire fits into. A pulley is used to lift or move things.

ramp: an inclined plane

screw: a sloping surface that winds in a spiral around a shaft. A screw is used to fasten or move things.

simple machine: a machine that operates without electricity and is used to make work easier. A simple machine changes the power, speed or direction of a movement.

wedge: an object with a wide end and a pointed or sharp edge. A wedge is used to split or separate things.

wheel and axle: a wheel or set of wheels fastened to a bar or rod. A wheel and axle is used to move things or change the power, speed or direction of a movement.

Index